Reflections from Harmony Hall

The Glenleigh

Reflections from Harmony Hall

A Collection of Poems

Vilma C. Morales Daley

To order additional copies of this book, contact:
Xlibris Corporation
1-888-795-4274
www.Xlibris.com
Orders@Xlibris.com
104327

Contents

NATURE

RELIGIOUS

TO PARENTS

WOMEN, RELATIONSHIPS, AND SOCIETY

To my mother, my first teacher who read many books and poems to me during my childhood years. Also to the memory of my late father, Alvin George Morales, who worshiped with the family every morning before breakfast and taught us to love God, ourselves and our neighbor.

Acknowledgments

Special thanks to my mother, Lesline Morales, who named me "Vilma Clare," but often addressed me as "Lady Clare" and who always had high expectations of me and my siblings. Her love for poetry has had a strong impact on me.

Thanks to my late father, Alvin George Morales, who told all his daughters that they were princesses and treated each accordingly. My Father's love for our Mom was evident to all, and he insisted on a high quality life for us. Dad sang love songs to mom, told us jokes that had lessons about life and danced with us. Thanks for his many lyrics.

Thanks to my sisters—Yunena, Olwen, Angella, Dona, Jeniffer, Marlon Rose Marie, and Audra for challenging me and for expressing joy in listening to my poems.

Thanks to my brothers, Milton, Norman, and Alvin, who accompany me each year to the "Calabash" literary festival and for the laughter we share.

My gratitude to Mr. Alfred Whittaker for permission to use the picture of "The Glenleigh" property on the cover of this publication

Thanks to Mr. Collin Binning for providing the photographs of "Glenleigh" and for all his assistance. Thanks also to my friend, Rosaline Windross Salmon, for supporting my efforts.

Sincere thanks to Mrs. Yvonne Hyacinth Darby Gilkes for her friendship and constant encouragement to publish my poems.

Thanks to my son Gregory, who designed the front cover of this book and for assisting me with my general use of technology. Most of all, I thank him for being a wonderful, caring son.

Thanks to my husband Dalbert, with whom I share my daily journeys.

It is with gratitude that I acknowledge the wonderful team at Xlibris for their input with this publication.

Foreign Words, Biblical and other terminologies

¡Adelante!	Forward!	(Spanish)
Va' avanti	Forward!	(Italian)
Avancez	Forward!	(French)
Vorwärts	Forward	(German)
leviathan	Job 41:1	
	Ps74:14	
	Isa 27:1	

The Piped Piper of Hamelin by Robert Browning

Psalm 27

A Psalm of David

(my mother's favorite Psalm)

The Lord is my light and my salvation;
Whom shall I fear?
The Lord is the strength of my life;
Of whom shall I be afraid?
When the wicked,
Even mine enemies and my foes,
Came upon me to eat up my flesh,
They stumbled and fell.
Though an host should encamp against me,
My heart shall not fear:
Though war should rise against me,
In this will I be confident.
One thing have I desired of the Lord,
That will I seek after;
That I may dwell in the house of the Lord
All the days of my life,
To behold the beauty of the Lord,
And to enquire in his temple.
For in the time of trouble
He shall hide me in his pavilion:
In the secret of his tabernacle shall he hide me;
He shall set me up upon a rock.
And now shall mine head be lifted up
Above mine enemies round about me:

Therefore, will I offer in his tabernacle sacrifices of joy;
I will sing, yea, I will sing praises unto the Lord.
Hear, O Lord, when I cry with my voice:
Have mercy also upon me, and answer me.
When thou saidst, seek ye my face;
My heart said unto thee, Thy face, Lord, will I seek.
Hide not thy face far from me;
Put not thy servant away in anger:
Thou hast been my help; leave me not, neither forsake me,
O God of my salvation.
When my father and my mother forsake me,
Then the Lord will take me up.
Teach me thy way, O Lord, and lead me in a plain path,
Because of mine enemies.
Deliver me not over unto the will of mine enemies:
For false witnesses are risen up against me,
And such as breathe out cruelty.
I had fainted, unless I had believed
To see the goodness of the Lord in the land of the living.
Wait on the Lord: be of good courage,
And he shall strengthen thine heart:
Wait, I say, on the Lord.

Psalm 23

A Psalm of David

(my father's favorite Psalm)

The Lord is my shepherd;
I shall not want.
He maketh me to lie down in green pastures:
He leadeth me beside the still waters.
He restoreth my soul:
He leadeth me in the paths of righteousness
For his name's sake.
Yea, though I walk through the valley
Of the shadow of death,
I will fear no evil: for thou art with me;
Thy rod and thy staff they comfort me.
Thou preparest a table before me
In the presence of mine enemies:
Thou anointest my head with oil;
My cup runneth over.
Surely goodness and mercy shall follow me
All the days of my life:
And I will dwell in the house of the Lord for ever.

Love Songs

Alvin and Leslene Morales

Ode to My Father

(my hero)

Undiscovered, unknown genius
Of my childhood years,
Like ancient philosophers,
And bards of years long past,
Your satires, fables, and folktales,
Will forever last
In hearts titillated with your laudable lyrics,
Coined to dispel tears and fears,
Didactic in nature, thought provoking
Yet laughter evoking,
Your wisdom beyond measure
Audiences for more, are always yearning.

Steadfast and prudent,
Honest and always giving,
Your vision and cadence
With me, will remain
As long as I'm living.
And to our mom, what tributes of love!
The sharing and caring
As if to a gentle dove.

Your children too,
With the glories of fatherhood were blessed,
For truly of such joys, can surely confess.
So let the world know,
Today I proclaim you
In sonnets and continuous refrains,
Father laureate, indeed, it is true.

Ode to My Mother

(my patron saint)

In summer's salient sunshine
Beaming brightly,
I think of you
For, like the forever forging
And reaching rays,
You warm my heart too.
In winter's foreboding frost,
On you my thoughts remain
For your saintly smiles
And loving ways
Are like the promise of summer's refrain

And when avid, autumn days appear,
I smile and think of how you love to share
The blessed gifts to you that God has given
And autumn's blanket of fallen leaves unhidden
Remind me of the lessons in faith and truth
Which you delicately and strategically instilled
From days of youth

The millions of tiny, twinkling stars
In the night sky above
Remind me of the luster
Of your unfailing love
And beckon my recall
Of the many times
From you I gained strength,
Especially when you said,
Put your hands in the hands of the Lord
Upon Him, you must be bent

The Pacific Ocean

Beyond the sand dunes I see you
Creating continuous, temporary formations
Of liquid, rippling mountains.
Flaunting your foaming, frothing exhibits
Of lacy layered patterns
Displaying the illusions
Of ladies luring petticoats in playful moves
Dashing, lashing, dipping, and seething
Your delight belies the monotony
Of the gentle, flowing fountain.

Ascending to unimaginable heights,
As if to remind us to keep looking above,
Your leaping, bounding and bending
Create a liturgical dance-
Divinely choreographed
With performance in rhythmic reticence,
And yet at times, billowing boisterously
Still prayerfully,
Yielding vibrations and rhythms
That heal and ease,
You challenge and you beckon,
You sing and you sway,
And you provide a peaceful
Choral roundelay.

On My Son's Birth

A bundle of joy
How blessed we are
Into our arms a dear little boy
Meek and cuddly, just like a lamb
Only the great God above
Could grant this gift so full of love

A living, breathing offspring to treasure
A gift beyond all concept of measure
With love, you'll shelter, nurture, and protect
And help you to develop your intellect
Patience, understanding I'll give you my best
And as you grow in faith
Of you, I really will expect no less.

Oh! Father of love
Give us wisdom
His life to guide
To You, heavenly Father
Our son we dedicate,
Give him wisdom
Your love, Your peace, Your grace
And to Your will
May he never hesitate!

This day, I'll always remember
There came my son so warm and tender,
And always will it be on my agenda
As long as I'm living,
To give homage and thanksgiving
On this day so full of love and glee.

Our Wedding Day

A Song of Love

(for Dalbert)

I want to be gently
And lovingly swept up
In the gleeful energy
Of your copious love
I want to hold your hand
As the moonlight
Directs its glow
And spotlights us
In solitude and warm embraces
While still captivating our gestures
In guarded silence
For moonlight does provide
Silhouettes of lovers
Creating nature's temporary videos

I want to count the stars with you
And watch them twinkle endlessly
I want to be assured
That our love, like the stars above
Will forever sparkle brightly
I want to know
That nothing, nothing
Will ever extinguish
The commingled heat
And the fiery ambers
That keep aglow our love

I want to hear the songs of love
That undeniably tell our own story
And refresh and replenish
The melodies and rhythms of our souls
I want to dance with you
The dances that life has to offer
And know that you will keep the beat
And listen to the tunes
As we move together in synchrony and harmony
To life's classic overtures
And sweet love songs

Oh! May such music
Be the prelude to our journey
As we walk together
Hand in hand

Sonnets of My Soul

(for my siblings)

Sonnets of my soul
Give rise to joyous canticles
Of bonds unbreakable
Germinated by my parents' love
United by sacrament true and holy

Nurtured and cradled
Within the comfort
Of my mother's womb
In the sanctity divinely crafted
In my mother's womb

The true God above
Has continually extended
His blessings and love
Same flesh, same blood
Same genes, a true gift from above

Siblings
Of the same eternal source
A billion troupes
Cannot us divide
For united we stand
United in spirit and in love

Across oceans, hand in hand we remain
Over continents, our unity prevails
Sometimes in pain, anger, or frustration
Yet love, from its roots
Never takes leave

How blessed are we
To share so much
Oh, great God
Let us each stand firm in You, Lord
Remembering Your constancy and love
Remaining united in faith
United in spirit
Siblings of the same eternal source

Oh Rome!

Oh, ancient imperial land
Land of the seven hills
Land of the Vatican City
Housing distinct relics and treasures
That bear witness
To the foundation of my parent's faith
Passed down to me!
Through generations untold

Land where among many
Michelangelo, Raphael,
Bernini, and Bramante
Left indelible physical works of artistry
Engraved in hearts
Touched by the Father's love

Oh, ancient land
With gardens, museums,
Arches, and basilicas
Land where beauty reigns
Here, the magnificence
Of the Coliseum decaying lies
Telling voiceless stories of past glories
And St. Peter's Basilica
In its magnificence
No few words can describe

Oh, land of the many towering obelisks
Symbols of immortality
Pointing to the hovering sky
Providing landmarks for meeting place
For today's city guides
The catacombs too
Near the Appian Way
Where the crucified Christ
To Peter did appear
Provide insight
Of organized historical disposal
Of Christian dead

And the many elegant fountains
How marvelous to behold
But to the Trevi Fountain
I'll hurry today
My back I'll turn
A coin I'll toss in
For to Rome
To beautiful, unforgettable Rome
I must, I simply must return.

Gregory E. A. Daley

Gregory E. A. Daley

A Song for My Son

I hear sweet music playing
Sweet music bringing delight to my ears
It's the ascending sound
One rung at a time
Of your footsteps on the stairs
As they announce your presence
And joy fills my heart
Joyous rills, throughout my body fill

I hear sweet music playing
Sweet music bringing delight to my ears
It's the dangling of your keys
Clinging, jingling, and together clanging
And spontaneously
From deep within my being
A smile in jubilation
Captures every muscle of my face
You're home, and joy fills my heart
Joyous rills, throughout my body fill

I hear sweet music playing
Sweet music bringing delight to my ears
It's the bold declaration—
The unlocking of the door
A declaration of your entitlement
What delight to see your face again
A whole day has come to an end
And safely home you've made it
A sigh of relief and thanksgiving
Yes, Lord! I do not take it for granted
And joy fills my heart
Thank You Lord, Thank You!

POEMS AS FOOD FOR THOUGHT

The Deceitful One

Like wolf in sheep's clothing you came
My friend to be, you gloriously proclaimed
And passionately my confidence you did seek
While unknowingly and being too credulous
I did concede,
And to you, my innermost secret thoughts
I revealed.
But as swift as the flames of a raging fire,
You made public, my secret thoughts and desires.

Oh, justice, deny not this disguised leviathan
Your esteemed power.
Oh, justice, waver not your knout this hour.
Had I but Prometheus's inborn gift,
From your skittish and egregious plan
I would desist,
For you are no different from that which
Beneath the rocks
Lurks and slithers,
Then upon your victim, you lash
A life-threatening sting
To make him cower.
Deny it not, for it is true,
No living thing than you
Is lower.

Harlem Renaissance

Rise up, rise up, and be aware!
Can't you see, can't you see?
Can't you instinctively perceive the snare
From those who once scuffed at you?
From those who previously
Would never be in Harlem streets
Except on bus tours?

Where will you go?
What will you do now?
The mat has from under your feet
Been removed
Your future by the villains
Was long planned

But why were you so long asleep?
And why do you so complacent seem?
Rise up I say!
Rise up, too late, it's not!
Rise up, regroup, and take control
Of the blessed acreage
To you by God above bestowed!

Your fathers and forefathers
With pride through those ancient doors
Gained the right to vote
They earned respect—
Don't go back, Oh no!

Your soul to the devil
Do not sell!
In years to come
Through those Harlem streets
Your children will dare not walk
With casual steps and freely pass
Without scrutiny and contempt
From those to whom
Their birthright you sold!

Rise up, rise up I say!
Your destiny is in your own making
Rise up, rise up
Don't give up, I pray
Don't passively watch this gentrification
This will lead to your demise
And destabilization
Rise up, and take action

Be a team, join forces
Be a living proof
That action and reaction
Can renew a city
Can renew the human spirit
Raise your hands and spirits
In one accord

Raise your hands to the God above
For strength and deliverance
Because you know and I know
That only through Him
Are all things possible.

A Song of Truth

Don't try to harness my vocal discourses
For no restraints can befuddle
Or withhold my sources
No insidious and capricious acrimony
Can contain or silence me honey!
For truth is the ocean from which flows
The source of my utterances
And overflows within me
Like the flooding banks
Of a river in spate

Oh, let me indulge and experience
The depths of its spontaneity
And validate the roots of my humanity
For I cannot contain this powerful urge
To vent and express
This tumultuous surge
Creates upheaval within me
Protesting the attempts to silence me

This force within me
Is like that which issues forth
The fiery red lava and molten rocks
Oozing down the orifice of untamed ravines
And I will not be silenced!

I will not stand by quietly
I will stand firm and vociferous
The world will hear my cry and know me
For venting is cleansing
So let me emit
The impurities that may hinder me
Yes, I will not be quieted
I will stand firm and free
Free, knowing that I honored
My constitutional rights.

Metamorphosis of Wrath

The storm has subsided
The calmness and peacefulness now
Bear no trait
Of the painful pangs
And relentless uproar
That devastate and rob
And send fearful tremors
Through human souls

All is still now
And only those who experienced it
Know truly the agony of such rage
Words never really reinvent
The exact image of the story of wrath

Those who experience it
Know that wrath has no empathy
No piety, no soul, no compromise, no sense
Wrath has no friend
No sense of dignity
No unity, no ideals, no grace, no morals
Wrath is truly devoid of God's bountiful
love

Then strangely, unpredictably
Abruptly, after the flare
After the raw vengeance
After the continuous raging
And vehement fluid anger

Wrath takes leave
As if clothed in innocence
With no face to cover in shame

Uptown Child

Uptown child
I'm talking to you
Pay attention!
Don't project this on anyone else

You're marking time
Dad would say
Adelante! Va' avanti
Forward march!
Life and progress
Must be synonymous
Graduated summa cum laude
From a school of distinction
Now show your "stuff"!

Avancez, Vorwärts
Knowledge without application
Is simply vain
So long delayed
Your progress has been
What's your justification?
Why the apprehension?

Oh, tell me
You privileged uptown child
Life is valuable, and life is short
No time for nonchalance
Nor passive stance
Oh, beautiful child
Collect yourself
Find your strength
Forget excuses
Apply yourself!

You've been blessed
Beauty and all the rest
And time on no one waits

So with passion, child
Now proceed
Everyone is counting on you
You can do it!
You can do it!
You can do it!
You were born for it!

My Wish for You

Liberate yourself
From the confining cubicles
Of self-pity and self-limitations
In which you have imprisoned yourself
And obviously your mind!
Liberty provides opportunities for growth
Oh how I wish you would liberate yourself.

Look far beyond
The limited parameters
Self-imposed
Now joyfully see
The glories stretching forth
In the glowing horizon
Oh! how I wish you would liberate yourself.

Bask in the hope of the rising sun
Claim your God-given right
To an earned share in prosperity
Blue skies are ahead
Success awaits you
Oh! I hope you will liberate yourself!

Freedom

Freedom! Freedom!
For freedom you call—
But freedom comes not from mighty kings
Nor from empty walls
Freedom comes not from bejeweled
And quest-driven queens
Freedom comes when we can truly unlock
The superficial boundaries of our inner being
And know that God, we cannot mock

Freedom comes when we protect each other
As friend and brother
And walk in dignity with love for one another
Freedom comes when we teach our children
To take their rightful place
As members of a chosen race
And empower them with the laws
Our forefathers held dear
Then they will walk head held high
Without fears

Freedom, though every man's right, I declare
Will never come through blaming and retaliating
Freedom comes through wisdom
From the Almighty, who is always fair
For the weapons that secure our freedom
Are those we have in hindsight long laid down

And oh, how much we could overcome
If we ardently work for God's kingdom
There are many who believe they are free
But surely, they are only slaves
For if we enslave another
Oh gee! We too are slaves
Not like men of ancient days
But slaves to the chronic need
To deprive another man of his God-given gifts

And so, shouldn't we choose to love and uplift?

Dances

Dance no more
I will with you
Dances have rules,
Dances have procedures
You too must follow
If in synch we must be

When I follow the rules
And you dance freestyle
There is discord
And the rhythm is lost
Dance no more
I will with you

No choreography will you accept
And I want to tame
That stubborn, defiant spirit
That beguiles the beauty
And the gracefulness of this dance

This dance was intended
To be consistent and fluid
So as we glide and skip across the hall
We should hold hands and feel uplifted
And full of pride
Because we added genius
And grace and mastery to this dance

Tell me now
Will you pause
Listen, understand, and try?
Will we dance apart
In distant places
Or will sweet memories
Be made to forever last?

The Antidote

I wish I could find the antidote
To erase or even differ
The maladies of old age
The maladies that affect
Or detract from
Man's exterior youthful features
And revert independent
Reliable people of all races
Into the child they once had been

Oh! I wish I could find the antidote
That would remove
The Shakespearean dewlaps
From my aging fellowman's drooping face
And replace the flaccid furrows
So deeply embedded
With newfound grace

Oh! I wish I could find the antidote
That would prevent
Age-old bones from breaking
And cure vision and hearing loss
These maladies for the aging population
Would surely be a thing of the past

At Christmas time.
I'd wrap this antidote
In multitudes of packages so pretty and fine
I'd leave this gift at the door
Of every aging citizen for sure
I would bequeath the balance to my only dear son
For I know he'd keep passing it on

Oh! I wish I could find the antidote
To erase the chronic pains
That come with the golden years
I'd really like to make this change
To bring happiness and relief
From fears so strong and yet so real.

Twisted Truth

The truth
Twisted—
Mangled like wires
Disconnecting and disallowing
Continuous positive flow of energy
Energy needed
For life-supporting machinery
The machinery for cultural uniformity
The machinery for social wholeness
This twisted truth, banefully contorted
With indomitable fallacies
Will bring tears

This twisted truth
Fed to the youth
Even to babies
As they lactate comfortably
In the arms and embraces
Of parental comfort
Comfort divinely provided
This twisted truth
Put forth to teach hate
Dissension, and separation
Has been fed
To generations upon generations

This fabrication
That skin color makes a person
Less or more than another is dangerous.
How evil! How sinister
To purposely mislead our children!
The children of whom Jesus said
"Let the little ones come unto me"
How audacious to mislead them,
How malicious, How fraudulent?
How unfathomable
To intoxicate young minds
With pernicious fallacies!
The truth about God's children
With skins tones
Celebrated by gentle
And sometimes bold kisses from the sun
Will come to light

And tell me!
Do you really love
The children you teach to hate?
Well, how do you define love?
Know now
That to nurture God's little angels
Upon hate and deceit
Is to turn away from God

Remember
When the Piped Piper returns
And he will return
To eradicate the vermin
That gnaw away
On the delicate fibers
Interwoven for congruence
And unity and decency
In society.
This time
The children will not be led away!
The payment
For the wrongs they were taught
Will not be on their heads
This time
Their innocence will set them free

This time
Those who misled them
Those who misguided them
Those who separated and hated
And lied and misconstrued
This time
They will be led away
Unless they redeem themselves
This time
They will face the music
They will follow
Into the deep perilous water
And the truth will prevail.

Nature

The Songbird

I know the song of the sweet singing bird
To me, it brings comfort when clearly heard
Deeply sacred for me, the story it conveys
For comfort in my heart, it never betrays
I know the song of the sweet-singing bird

Of great importance
Are the unknown words
The tune may be the same
But in each human heart
The words do change
Yes! Each heart like a drum
Pulsating to its own beat
Or murmuring hum
I know the song
Of the sweet-singing bird.

This tune does, in my heart, linger on
A tune I can never shun
One that inspires within me
A sacred response
And tempers and enhances
My inner being,
Even from a distance
I know the song of the sweet-singing bird

Like the song in my heart
That quiets my soul

So too is your song,
You beautiful bird
The words, no one knows
Except for sure
He whom we all adore
I know the song
Of the sweet-singing bird

Rivers

Rivers of love, uniting the world
Rivers of peace, touching our souls
Rivers of joy, bringing friendship to all
Rivers winding and meandering
Rippling rivers, dancing in daylight
Creating soft music for all to enjoy

Rivers flowing inside you and me
Through hills and dales
Rivers of fresh flowing air
Rivers of darkness when nighttime falls
Rivers of light
Flowing through the windows of the world

Rivers, life supporting channels
Rivers that transport
Rivers that irrigate
Rivers producing power to light our world
Rivers for baptisms, cleansing even our souls.

Brothers and sisters
Let's keep all rivers clean
Just to enhance our well being
Clean rivers for you and for me
Keeping balance to our eco-system you see
Healthy habits will surely bring us gain
And alleviate a great deal of pain
Clean, fresh flowing rivers
Do reflect, the mores and values of a people
Rivers, reflecting rivers
Clean rivers are rivers of love.

RELIGIOUS

The Angelus Bells

Why do I no longer hear
The sweet melodious sounds
Of the holy Angelus bells so dear?
They would each day resound
From steeples so high above
Oh! Those delightful bells
Bells of my childhood years of love
Are still ringing in my heart so well

Ring out you bells, ring out
I must stop everything now
And kneel and respond in love
In prayer too my head I'll bow
To recall the coming of the Gentle Dove
In God's greatness, I'll rejoice and pray
As Mary magnified the Lord above
Her part she played without delay

Ring out, you joyous bells, ring out
Three times during the day
Six hours apart
Sweet Angelus bells would ring and play
Their unifying sounds
Are still echoing now
Those dainty, delightful sounds would abound
And were always heard throughout the town

Ring out, you joyous bells, ring out
Joyously touching you and me
Recalling the story ever so true
Of the angel who Mary did see
The news, the world to renew
Announcing the Savior's coming

Those synchronous bells
They keep me always humming
With joy this music swells

First Communion

(for Emily)

A day to remember
This day to forever savor
It's First Communion
On a bright Sunday morn
And I am so blessed
And so well adorned
I'm happy, oh, so happy
To be the beneficiary
Of this Holy Gift
From a sweet-loving Savior
Who always bestows
His kindness and ceaseless care

Come now wherever from!
Come Dad and come Mom!
Come aunts, uncles, cousins, and friends
Come witness this joyous religious event
Christ gave His life to redeem and cleanse
Today at His holy banquet
At the church's request
For the first time ever
I'll feast at His table so blessed
Bread made flesh
To cleanse and refresh
Wine into blood
Our life to redeem
My part I'll play
The world to reform
With God by my side
Many good deeds I'll perform

Confirmation Day

(for Gregory)

Holy Spirit enfold you
Your faith to renew
Christian maturity and enlightenment
New powers and fulfillment
Cleansing fire like showers
On Pentecost day,
Oh! What powers
Come Holy Spirit,
Come right now, Your blessings to bestow.

Consecrated on Holy Thursday
Oil of chrism here today
Anointing grace in this holy place
Fruit of the Holy Spirit
Only God can give it
Read the Bible, He lives
Come, Holy Spirit
Come right now, empower us with Your gifts

Powerful gift
Miracles to perform
Only if you truly believe
Holy Spirit sanctified, this to conceive
Sanctified and blessed, head to toe
Now washed in His blood you know
Come Holy Spirit,
Come right now, our lives to reform

Empowering God's children
A gift so complete
Once in a lifetime to receive
Go forward in love
Chosen, confirmed, and blessed
A new light now shines
And you will bear it
Now and always
Come Holy Spirit,
Come right now and seal us with your grace

My Guardian Angel

I need you beside me
When cold harsh winds blow
And there's no solar heat
And no fires aglow
I need you beside me
When the dark night falls
And accentuates the screech owl's call
I need you beside me
When I'm in a foreign land
So puzzled by cultures unknown
And my only comfort;
The thought of you
I need you beside me
To share my sorrows and my joys
I need you beside me
To remind me of the strength I have
Deeply veiled within my being
A reservoir of empowerment
A gift divine,
A gift full of love.
I need you
For you are my angel
Sent from above.

TO PARENTS

Discipline 101

(for a child in need of behavior modification)

Don't wait to call "Super Nanny"
Don't wait for "Child Welfare Services"
Face the facts and tell the truth
Your child is very rude
Don't cover up his wrongs
He will cause you to be ashamed
Stop saying that it is because
Someone else did something wrong
That resulted in your child's misbehavior

I don't want to see you crying
And beating up yourself, asking
"Lord, where did I go wrong with this child?"
Don't cover up anymore
Take the child into council
Look him straight in the eyes
Remind him that
He is the child
And you are the adult

Remember that
He has no mental or emotional disorder
And nothing is wrong with his ears
So be strong and take control
From now on
Let him know who sets the rules
You are the mother
You are the father

He is the child
He does not have the authority
Nor the same privileges
That you, as adults have

Make sure he has no hearing problem
So you know he hears you very well
He has rights you must surely know
So don't infringe upon his dignity
Only remember that
God gave him to you for guidance
And you are responsible for this task
Discipline him with love and grace
Don't shout at him
Don't disrespect him
Don't swear at him

Tell him like it is
For he is very smart
He will understand
Don't underestimate him
With guidance
He will make you very proud

If the cap fits
Wear it

Discipline 101

(in Jamaican dialect)

Noh wait fi caal Super Nanny
Noh wait fi Child Welfare Services
Face di facts an tell di truth
Yuh pickney really rude
Noh cover up di wrang
Im wi shame yuh
Stop saying a cause
Smaddy else did sup'm
Dat cause im
Fi ack dat way
Mi noh waa fi si yuh bawl
And ole yuh belly a seh
"Lord! Where did I go wrong?"
Tek di pickney inna yuh han
Look im straight inna im eye
Remind im dat
Im a di pickney
An yuh a di adult
Memba dat
Im no av no mental
Or emotional disorder
So, be strang and tek control

Fram now aan
Let im know who set di rule
Yuh a di madda, an yuh a di faada
Im a di pickney
Im no av di autahrity
Nor di same privileges
Dat yuh di adult av
An stick no bruck inna im ears
Im av rights yuh mus agree
So no infringe upon Im dignity
Only memba dat
God give im to yuh fi guide
An yuh responsible fi dis task
Discipline im wid love an grace
No shout and bawl after im
Tell im like it is
For im is very smaat
Im whi undastand
No undaestimate im

"Mi trow mi cawn, Mi no cawl nuh fowl"

Twin Girls

(For a Special Friend)

Twin girls, twin girls
Like dainty delightful pearls
You asked for one
He gave you two
Double blessings
To you from above
How glorious to behold
The beauty of God's love
In these innocent eyes
Brightly beaming at us

Bless them Lord
We ask in prayer
In your light-
In wisdom too
May they always walk
Knowing You
The true God of all

A Baby Daughter

(for Hannah)

What joy!
What love!

A dear little girl
Hair so soft
With silky little curls

God's wonderful gift to us a daughter
To fill our days with love and laughter
Oh Great God, Your wonders never cease
Please fill her life with your love and peace

Give us wisdom
Her life to direct
And our baby from harm
We ask you to protect
To You, Oh God
Our daughter we dedicate
And from Your will
May she never stray.

WOMEN, RELATIONSHIPS, AND SOCIETY

She Told Me Why

I know why she ran away
She whom everyone condemns
I know why she left
Everything behind
Despised by so many others
Who swear she is a fool
To run from such good fortune
They wish they had

In this great house with gothic architecture
And antique fixtures so unique
Some even golden
Perched on top of a hill
Extending unspoken welcome
To only those specially invited
With golden retrievers
Issuing the echoes
Beware, beware, beware!

Perhaps you don't know how it is
To feel frozen in the hot summer sun
To feel whipped by icy breezes
When there is no breeze
To feel all alone when there is company
And everyone says, "She is so lucky"

I know why she ran away
Living a lie is self-consuming
For on the outskirts of her door
She is full of smiles
She must show the world
Her charm, her beauty, and her good fortune
But behind those closed doors
The limits and deceit
The treachery and powerlessness
Become too much to bear

For in love so sweet
Her joys she thought would last
But from her
Such joys were cunningly
Snatched away and passed
And in a daze to live and breathe
With sighs and groans through smiles

Now grown up, but forced to relive
A second time her toddler years
Striving once again for independence
Hoping for autonomy
Shadowed and shackled into enormous lies
She must to herself be truthful now
And seek that which adds quality to life

Don't ridicule her
For taking a chance at life
Instead, admire her, you must
Some seek power
Some seek wealth
Some seek happiness and some
Just want to be loved and respected
Even if she fails, she took action
Give her credit, her independence
And her individuality must be regained

No one leaves security and happiness
For the cold open unknown
If upon arising
There is warmth and tenderness
And respect for human dignity all around

Stretch out your hand tenderly
And help her achieve her goal
So when you let go
She can really smile
And stand on her own two feet
And experience the victory
Of overcoming the challenge
Of an imposed second childhood
And watch her walk victoriously
The road to adulthood once more

Healing

The pain is more than can be imagined
Words fail to express its depth
The intensity of the damage
Is like the devastation brought on
By a wild-wielding
And continuous Southern hurricane
Oh my soul is deeply disturbed!

Here flooding, foaming rivers
Create debris of everything in sight
With temporary, angry, cascading waterfalls
Gushing down embankments from innocent hills
Sweeping away the security and sanctity
Of lifelong treasures and human dignity
Oh my soul is deeply disturbed!

And massive boulders are riveted
From their anchors of thousands of years
Of security and tranquility
And thunderous, lightening bolts
Send shock waves
Of luminous fiery streaks
Dancing in mid-air
Oh my soul is deeply disturbed!

And the pain will not go away
And the hurt, like salt or lime or alcohol
In a newly inflicted wound
Triggers itself repeatedly
Constantly reviving itself
Oh my soul is deeply disturbed!

For the spiritual bond that united us
Through cherished years
Of sharing and caring
And brought delight and blissful moments
And etched upon my heart
A glorified vision for the future
Has been boldly tarnished
Like silver
From long intense periods of oxidation
But the jeweler's rouge
Is not an agent for hearts or souls
Oh my soul is deeply disturbed!

And now for the healing
I need to hear the words that flow
From a deeply contrite
And repentant heart
I need the simple honesty
That reminds me of the purity of a rose
For it is a rare rose
That is reflective
Of joys now appearing long past
Oh my soul is deeply disturbed!

I need the promise
Reflective of the rainbow
No tokens now, only caring and nurturing
A promise that today
A new homestead we've entered
Where only brave pioneers dare tread
To embark upon new beginnings—
Where only the strong and the brave
May tread and survive and endure
Oh my soul will then be revived!

Playful Feet

Some look at faces first
Some know
That feet can tell
The same story that faces express

Olive brown feet
Poised upon black stiletto heals
Backless
Thin, curvaceous
Petite green straps
Holding the sole
Become the uppers
Accentuating sensuous pointed toe shoes

Feet, recently given a pedicure, waxed, and oiled
Playfully rubbing against each other
One foot removed from the grasp of the uppers
Set free, teasing, and taunting
Slowly dancing to body rhythms and vibes
Then again
Playfully slipped back
Into black pointed toe shoes

Pivoting left then right
Back and forth
Flicking now
Continuously in and out
Tapping toes
That send messages
Messages of feminine yearnings

Messages of desires
To quench the thirst
Of nature's insidious tendencies
To be gratified and synchronized

Feet, shoes, tempting and teasing
Telling of sensuous desires
Feet, shoes
They tell so much